THE ART ROOM

Billy Aronson

BROADWAY PLAY PUBLISHING INC
New York
www.broadwayplaypublishing.com
info@broadwayplaypublishing.com

First published by B P P I in *Plays From Woolly Mammoth:* September 1999
This edition, slightly revised: May 2012
I S B N: 978-0-88145-529-8
Book design: Marie Donovan
Page make-up: Adobe Indesign
Typeface: Palatino
Printed and bound in the U S A

ABOUT THE AUTHOR

Billy Aronson's plays have been produced by
Ensemble Studio Theater, Playwrights Horizons,
Woolly Mammoth Theater, Wellfleet Harbor
Actors Theater, 1812 Productions, Amphibian Stage
Productions, City Lights Theater Company, and the
S F Playhouse; awarded a commission from the Magic
Theater, a grant from the New York Foundation for the
Arts, and an Outstanding Original Script prize from
the Bay Area Theater Critics Circle; and published in
5 volumes of *Best American Short Plays*. His writing
for the musical theater includes the original concept/
additional lyrics for the Broadway musical RENT,
and the book for the Theaterworks/U S A musical
CLICK CLACK MOO, which received a Lucille Lortel
nomination for Best Musical. His T V writing credits
include M T V's *Beavis & Butt-head*, Cartoon Network's
Courage the Cowardly Dog, and Nickelodeon's *Wonder
Pets*, for which he served as head writer and received
an Emmy Award. He lives in Brooklyn with his wife
Lisa Vogel and their offspring Jake and Anna. (www.
billyaronson.com)

THE ART ROOM was originally produced by Woolly Mammoth Theater Company, Washington, DC (Howard Shalwitz, Artistic Director; Kevin Moore, Managing Director), where it opened on 24 May 1999. The cast and creative contributors were:

NORMA .... Donise Stevens*
JACKIE .... Jennifer Mendenhall
JON .... Oliver Wadsworth
THOMAS .... Delaney Williams
MADELINE .... Maia DeSanti
ART .... Hugh Nees

Director .... Sara Chazen
Set design .... Robin Stapley
Costume design .... Lynn Steinmetz
Lighting design .... Jay Herzog
Sound design .... Dan Schrader
Properties .... Susan Senita Bradshaw
Stage manager .... Annica Graham

*The role of NORMA was later played by Lynn Steinmetz.

THE ART ROOM show sponsors were Alan Gilburg and Martha Spice, Laurie Kauffman and Hal Rogoff, and Sheldon and Barbara Repp.

THE ART ROOM had its New England premiere at the Wellfleet Harbor Actors Theater, Wellfleet, MA (Jeff Zinn, Artistic Director), where it opened on 12 June 2003. The cast and creative contributors were:

NORMA ....Lordan Niven Napoli
JACKIE ....Laura Latreille
JON ....Tommy Day Carey
THOMAS...Stephen Russell
MADELINE .... Kelly Mares
ART .... Charles Weinstein

Director .... Brendan Patrick Hughes
Set design ....Dan Joy
Costume design ....Robin McLaughlin
Lighting design ....Christopher Ostrom
Sound design... Ben Arons
Stage manager.. Sarah Locke

ACKNOWLEDGMENTS

Rewriting is dangerous! Especially when so much time has passed since the original inspiration (I wrote THE ART ROOM back in the 20th century!) But in recent years, seeing the play performed by different groups, I've become convinced that some cuts in the script would help. So when Kip Gould offered to publish a stand-alone edition of the play (he had already published it in *Plays From Woolly Mammoth*) I thought this would be the perfect opportunity to make some changes.

Thanks to the talented artists involved in those recent performances for educating and inspiring me:

*Jennifer Makholm and the Process Group Theater Company: Bryan Close, Ann Farrar, Tovah Suttle, Brian Lafontaine, Matt Savins, Heidi Armbruster, Erik Heger;

*Renee Pastel and her ensemble at Harvard: Julia L. Renaud, Christine Bendorf, Sarah Sherman, Michael Wolfe, Ben Cosgrove, Zia Okocha, and Michael Finnerty;

*Richard Gershberg and the Turbulence Theater Company: Kirsten Brant, Sarah Dandridge, Steven Lavner, Sheila O'Malley, Brett Penney, and John Stonehill.

Thanks also to those who contributed their passion and skill to the original development of the play:

*At Ensemble Studio Theatre: Jamie Richards, Sheri Matteo, Thomas Lyons, William Hill, Ellen Marenek, Dan Maher, Melinda Page Hamilton, and Chris Smith;

*At Primary Stages: Casey Childs, Brenda Cummings, Mike Connor, Dan Ahearn, Abigail Revasch, Scott Hudson, and Tracy Thorne.

Thanks to everyone at Woolly Mammoth Theatre and Wellfleet Harbor Actors Theatre who worked on the premiere productions.

And thanks to the remarkable Kip Gould for publishing plays!

CHARACTERS

NORMA, *mental ward attendant*
JON, *pathological liar*
JACKIE, *introvert*
THOMAS, *adult with the mind of a child*
MADELINE, *actress having a nervous breakdown*
ART, *businessman*

SCENES

The action takes place in the mental health ward of a hospital, over the course of a single day.

ACT ONE. Common room. Morning.

ACT TWO. Scene 1. Art room. Afternoon.

ACT TWO. Scene 2. Common room. Evening.

THE ART ROOM was inspired by Georges Feydeau's
TAILLEUR POUR DAMES.

ACT ONE

(The common room in a mental ward)

(A door leads to the hall. Doors on either side lead to bedrooms. Another door leads to a closet.)

(NORMA, dressed in hospital worker uniform, carrying a tray of pills, stands in a trance.)

NORMA: What the hell was I thinking. I wanted to get out of my depression. So I came to work in a mental ward. That's like trying to get rid of your fever by crawling into an oven. The people here fill up their days with little art projects and inane chores the doctors assign them. Jon checks the other patients for head lice. Jackie buffs the floor with a sock. All day. Every day. But the most pathetic thing is Jon and Jackie got this idea they're married. They can hardly have a ten second conversation without one of them going into convulsions. And now it looks like Jon's sleeping around. He's not in his bed or hers. When Jackie finds out they'll need to bring out the restraints and give her a half dozen injections. Too bad I won't be in on the fun. After this shift I'm out of here. Freedom. My life has been transformed by a tooth paste commercial. This woman in the ad is invincible because of her smile. All around her guys fall off ladders but she just walks right through. Blue silk scarf fluttering in the breeze. Toothy smile sparkling in the sun. In my desperate state the image seemed profound. So I did

like the toothpaste woman. Put a bounce in my step.
Bought a dozen blue silk scarves. And started smiling.
Constantly. When people asked how I was instead of
describing my depression I smiled. Then they smiled.
Soon I was surrounded by a bunch of smiling people.
But when the smiling people asked about my work,
then what. Didn't want to say I provide inadequate
assistance to people with terrible illnesses for a
degrading salary. So I said I'm applying for a fancy
bank job. And I applied for one. And I got it. I'll have
clients. Assistants who treat me like a grownup. And
a love life. Guy saw me smiling like an idiot. Couldn't
resist. He's totally different from other guys I've been
with. He's sane. It's a stretch for me, I know. But it's
been such a long dry spell I'm willing to overlook the
fact that he's reliable and fun to be with. He's picking
me up this afternoon and taking me to his place
upstate for the weekend. Would have been nice to
have made a dent here. Cured people. Ended human
suffering as glorious music poured down from the sky.
But I'm getting myself out of bed in the morning. A
miracle in its own right.

(The door on the right opens. Out crawls: JACKIE, *buffing
the floor with a sock.)*

NORMA: Morning Jackie. Chilly out today. Salisbury
steak on the dinner menu. Pill time.

*(*JACKIE *stops moving, starts again.)*

NORMA: Mashed potatoes too. You like mashed
potatoes, right? Come get your pills.

*(*JACKIE *stops moving.)*

NORMA: I like that sculpture you made out of all those
things you collected. I saw it under your bed. You've
got a real talent. Jackie?

*(*JACKIE *says something faintly.)*

NORMA: What's that?

(JACKIE *says something only slightly louder.*)

NORMA: Volume.

JACKIE: D'yuh give Jon his pills?

NORMA: I always give Jon his pills.

JACKIE: Yuh always give Jon pills before yuh give me pills.

NORMA: It's time to take *your* pills.

JACKIE: He take his?

NORMA: Jon gets medication every morning, you know that.

JACKIE: His door's closed.

NORMA: That it is.

JACKIE: Every morning yuh knock on Jon's door. Give Jon pills. Leave door open. Sometimes wide open. Sometimes just a crack. Always open.

NORMA: Well, no one always does everything in the exact same order Jackie. The important thing is—

(JACKIE *lobs her sock at* NORMA. *Beat. She leaps up and embraces* NORMA.)

JACKIE: I'm so so sorry.

NORMA: It's one of those days, huh.

(JACKIE *takes her pills.*)

NORMA: That's better. There you go. I'll make my rounds.

JACKIE: But the thing is—and yeah I do like mashed potatoes—all the parts of somebody's body are with my Jonny's body. The pores. The hairs. The lips yuh know. And I'm here. This is my body. My body needs to be with what's going on but it just can't be because I don't got the, the stuff inside me the ingredients.

NORMA: Jackie.

JACKIE: There's nothing inside me. But it takes up so much space. *(She holds her chest, gasps for air, crawls into her room, slams the door.)*

NORMA: Always nice to be of help.

(There's a banging on the door to the hall. NORMA *lets in:)*

*(*JON, *wearing a necktie. He darts around in a frenzy, taking his medication a little at a time.)*

JON: Everything's locked. You want to go somewhere, you try the door, but does it open? No, it's locked. Lock lock locked.

NORMA: The locks are only a problem for patients who go wandering at night.

JON: Did Jackie notice?

NORMA: She noticed.

JON: Noticed what. There was nothing to notice. What the hell was she doing noticing things.

NORMA: She knows you were out.

JON: I wasn't. I was in there the whole time. I'm in there now. Dead asleep. You tried to wake me. Gave up. Felt ashamed. Feared you were losing your wake-up-ability. So you shut the door on this blemish on your record. Slammed it tight. Walked away. Hush hush. But now I'm up and I'm talking so it's time to come clean.

NORMA: If you leave the room during the night again they're going to have to start locking you in.

JON: Then how can I see Madeline?

NORMA: Who's Madeline?

JON: New patient in "B" ward. Had a breakdown. Luckily for her.

NORMA: So you're—

JON: Craving this once-in-a-lifetime fantasy human with splendor screaming from her flesh.

NORMA: Ah.

JON: An actress, she is. Smile that makes you float, weep, smash your skull. This thespian has the potential to make me one profoundly contented Jonny.

NORMA: You don't look contented.

JON: Of course I don't look contented now, do I, because I spent the night in a closet, didn't I, because at midnight she was supposed to unlock the door to the ward, but it was locked at midnight and it was locked at twelve thirty-seven and twelve fifty-two and twelve fifty-nine and one and two and three and four and stop thinking what you're thinking you can just shut up, she does want me. She lets me tell her things. Lets me give her gum. She's not a good rememberer, that's all. But she's a good wanter. And she wants me.

NORMA: What about Jackie.

JON: That's not forever. Everybody knows that's not forever. It was never meant to be forever.

NORMA: I think you said it was forever.

JON: It was never forever.

NORMA: Fine.

JON: Jackie's fine. She's great. But she'll always be, you know, just, what she is. But I've got that certain, you know, I mean look at me. I've got all this burning... stuff, to share, to build...with someone else who has the stuff to share and build.

NORMA: Before you get sharing and building with the actress you better explain to Jackie.

JON: Of course of course I'll explain to Jackie, what d'you think I'd creep around like a weasely weasel? No no, I'll sit her down, tell her plain, spell it out.

NORMA: Uh huh.

JON: "These are my needs, those are your needs, I'm going in this direction, you're going in that direction—"

(JACKIE *crawls out.* JON *freezes up. Pause)*

NORMA: I'm going in this direction. *(She exits.)*

JON: Hey there. Morning. I saw something on T V. Or was it the papers. Big headline. Somebody took a stand. Somebody stood on my hand once. Thumbnail fell off. East west relations fell off in the fifties. Eisenhower, my god that guy was bald. Khrushchev too. Such power. And such baldness.

(JACKIE *speaks softly.)*

JON: Huh?

(JACKIE *speaks softly.)*

JON: Cat got your tongue? Oh there's this gigantic—

JACKIE: Where were yuh last night.

JON: There's this gigantic. Thing.

JACKIE: I just lay there. Whole night. Staring at the insides of my eyelids.

JON: Oh I was going to tell you about this huge platter of—I was in "C" ward. With Thomas.

(JACKIE *shakes her head.)*

JON: Head lice. Awful case.

JACKIE: Wearing a tie?

JON: I am thank you, yes. Granddad's. He passed away. We miss him dearly.

JACKIE: Yuh put on a tie to see Thomas?

JON: I did because the knot protects my Adam's apple from stray lice, no but seriously when I lean forward the tie hangs out due to gravity so it serves to keep me aware of not leaning in too close to the patient, really though the tie lends a nice appearance which tends to elevate the patient's overall mood.

JACKIE: So why didn't yuh come to bed after?

JON: How the hell could I, what am I a magician? I got the call, world's loudest knocking, can't believe you didn't hear it, ran over, ran back, grabbed my tie, ran back, and thank god I did because by the time I got to "C" ward the nits had blanketed Thomas' scalp. Sticky eggs on every strand. Tried to coax them with the comb but they clung. So I went for my glop. Glopped every follicle. Prayed the glop would take, but no luck. Thomas reached up to scratch, right through the glop, so I feared the worst, washed out the glop, scanned the scalp, and that's when I saw it: live hatched gnawing lice. Grabbed my poison pen, rammed the pellets into the fat face of each lousy louse. Thomas squealed like a pig. Clawed like a hawk. When he begged me to stop I had half a mind to head out, let nature do its worst, come crawling back to you. But let's not fool ourselves. If those lice took Thomas they wouldn't stop there. They'd sweep through the ward in a day, the wing in a week. Ever-mindful of the masses I summoned my last full measure of devotion, wrestled Thomas to the turf, gripped the poison pen in my throbbing palm and crushed every last one of the wee wiggly bastards. Round about dawn the scalp was still. Groggy but gratified I hobbled on home. If Thomas gets up before tomorrow I'll be shocked.

(THOMAS *enters.* JON's *body begins shaking.*)

THOMAS: Hi hi everybody.

JON: Thomas. Get back in bed. You're exhausted.

THOMAS: I feel really really good, because—

JON: You look disgusting, and no wonder.

THOMAS: Oh no no, I—

JON: You're wiped out. Dead.

THOMAS: He just makes me laugh and laugh.

JON: You weren't laughing last night.

THOMAS: Oh yes I was because, oh I can't wait to tell you—

JON: You came to thank me.

THOMAS: No no I want to—

JON: Oh I remember now, I told you to come back for the follow up.

(JON *checks* THOMAS' *head.*)

THOMAS: I really really can't wait to tell you about this dream.

JON: This won't hurt as much as last night, when I rushed over in the middle of the night—

THOMAS: You shouldn't wink at people if they're not winking at you. Ouch.

JON: Sorry but I've got to crush and crush the corpses, crush, crush.

THOMAS: You didn't see me last night, silly. Jon is a silly person.

(JACKIE *throws herself against a wall, goes out the door to the hall.* JON*'s body stops shaking.*)

JON: She's going to call her mother. Why did you have to show up.

THOMAS: Because I really really need to tell you about this dream I had.

JON: I've got to sleep.

THOMAS: Oh but what I have to say will be really really good for you because the dream made me so so happy that I woke up and thought how can I help all my friends and you're my best friend in the world because I really like you.

JON: Please go far away?

THOMAS: So I thought the best way I could help was, since I get to be in charge of all the keys to the whole sixth floor—

JON: The extra copies of the spare keys, that no human has ever actually needed.

THOMAS: I thought since some of the times nobody uses those rooms I could lend the keys to my friends.

JON: Why.

THOMAS: So like if you didn't want to check people's heads in their rooms or right here, you could use a room on the sixth floor like a real office.

JON: Your idea is moronic, which is a big step up for you since you're an idiot.

THOMAS: You like it?

JON: If by like you mean hate, yes. Now that you've told me what you came here to tell me—

THOMAS: Oh no no I came here mainly to tell you about my dream.

JON: I said—

THOMAS: I was sinking into the mud—

JON: I'm tired.

THOMAS: There was mud all around me—

JON: Shut up.

THOMAS: I was sinking down.

JON: Shut up.

THOMAS: I was stuck there.

JON: Shut. The.

THOMAS: I was sinking in the mud, when all of a sudden—

JON: Can't you understand? I do not want to hear your voice.

THOMAS: *(Whispers)* I was sinking in the mud—

JON: Oh god look at the time. I just realized there's a guy coming down to get checked.

THOMAS: Who?

JON: A new patient.

THOMAS: I really like new patients.

JON: Nobody likes this guy. He's unlikable.

THOMAS: What's his name?

JON: Boring. That's what they call him, and is he ever. Goes on and on.

THOMAS: Like me?

JON: Worse. He'd bore even you. So run.

THOMAS: But I really really want to tell you my dream now.

JON: And I really really wanted to hear it too. Oh well.

THOMAS: Oh well.

JON: Oh well.

THOMAS: Hey you want to hear a really good idea?

JON: No.

THOMAS: I'll stay in your bedroom for five minutes while you're checking Boring's head and then I'll come out and you can tell Boring "Oh look, it's this really boring guy, I just remembered I have to check his head," and then you'll be all free so you can hear my dream. Have fun with Boring. Tee hee.

(THOMAS *goes into* JON'*s bedroom.*)

JON: My room has been occupied by an idiot.

(JON *lies down on a table and closes his eyes.* JACKIE *returns.*)

JACKIE: I'm not the problem you're the problem.

JON: Your mother's coaching is the problem.

JACKIE: I do not have to be remained in the presence of by someone who is stepping on me viciously at all times.

JON: Jackie.

JACKIE: I would like you to dis-inhabit this area. That's just it. This chair, those chairs, the magazines, and all other property in this half. That's just what I'm saying.

JON: Jack.

JACKIE: Please remove your entire body from the air that is touching me. I do not wish to be in an atmosphere that contains you, things you see, the sight of you, or the sound.

JON: You're not going to trust Thomas' memory against my word—

(JACKIE, *silent scream*)

JON: You really didn't hear the knocking?

(JACKIE, *silent scream*)

JON: You're obviously upset.

JACKIE: I do not wish to have a liar so near my teeth. Stop from touching me now. Stop. Get.

JON: What's this really about.

JACKIE: These.

(JACKIE *takes pieces of wrapped chewing gum from her pajamas and throws them at him.* JON's *body starts shaking.*)

JACKIE: You don't chew gum.

JON: Great. You go through my things. They're not my things. Yes they are. But not in the way—that does it. Day after day I go out, touching heads, that might be crawling, and you're going to tell me I can't even test options, for protecting my fingers, new methods, such as gum wrappers.

(JON's *body stops shaking.*)

(JACKIE *shakes her head.*)

JON: Look at these fingers. What are they covered with? Hairs. What do lice get into? Hairs.

(JACKIE *shakes her head.*)

JON: What would you suggest I use? Dish gloves? Bulky, sopping—

JACKIE: Yuh could use hospital gloves.

JON: And deprive my patients of the minty scent?

(JACKIE *hisses at him, covers her face.*)

JON: Your mother did this to you. She hated me before she met me. You're trying to reason. Right? What's reasonable about hating someone first, then knowing them second?

JACKIE: I'm scared.

JON: Yes you're scared, your mother knows you're scared, and she uses that to make you more scared. Don't be scared.

JACKIE: I will.

JON: Isn't it better not to be scared?

JACKIE: No.

JON: You know it's better not to be scared.

JACKIE: No.

JON: You know it's better not to be scared.

JACKIE: Yeah.

JON: Then listen to me, don't be scared. Because you know how I feel.

JACKIE: No.

JON: You don't know how I feel?

JACKIE: No.

JON: You don't know how I feel? After all this time? Look at me. You really don't know how I feel? Should I scream? Should I run around? This is me. You know me. You know how I feel. I'll jump. Do you want me to jump, because I will. My whole body is about to jump. Look at me.

(JON *embraces* JACKIE. THOMAS *comes out.*)

THOMAS: She's not Boring. Hi Jackie, Jon said you were Boring but you're not Boring.

JACKIE: Too much people. Got to hibernate.

(JACKIE *goes into her room, closes the door.*)

JON: She's the best. But I've found someone who's more best, so I need one of those rooms you were talking about on the sixth floor.

THOMAS: Oh good—oh you can use the art room because it's just like a real doctor's office because it's got pretty paintings everywhere.

JON: Art...will keep my patient...relaxed...as I operate (*Laughs to himself*).

THOMAS: See how really happy you are? And it's all because of this dream I had that—

JON: Tell me as I inspect my new office.

(They start out the door, but hurry right back in. Jon's body shakes.)

JON: Madeline's coming. Get into my room.

THOMAS: I just was in your room.

JON: Get somewhere. Get here.

(JON shoves THOMAS into the closet, sits, picks up magazines, pretends to read, stops shaking.)

(MADELINE enters.)

THOMAS: *(From inside closet)* Can I tell you my dream from here?

JON: If you shut up until she goes you can tell me your entire dream eleven times.

THOMAS: *(From inside closet)* I really really can't wait.

MADELINE: I had the nicest walk over. The hall was open. The walls were still. The echoes steered clear of the shadows. But best of all was the light. It didn't buzz. Didn't pinch. Just washed right off my skin.

JON: It's great light for magazine reading, I can tell you that. Read read read, that's me. Suck the words right off the page.

MADELINE: I didn't know my husband was going to stay over last night.

(JON doesn't look up.)

MADELINE: He kept saying he was about to go home.

(JON doesn't look up.)

MADELINE: He's still in the building, so I told him I was coming to have my head checked for lice.

JON: Spearmint?

(JON offers gum, MADELINE takes.)

(MADELINE chews, JON paces. She dozes, he creeps close. She jerks awake, he resumes pacing. She spits, he sits.)

JON: There's more where that came from.

MADELINE: I'm sorry if you waited for me last night—

JON: No I'm sorry because I'm the one who couldn't make it. Up all night with my magazines. Got way behind. *(Reads)* "Frequent Death. Massive Slide. President Pushes Congress." The nerve.

MADELINE: But doesn't it make you dizzy?

JON: Sure. What.

MADELINE: The magazines have a story. It comes to life. It's about your world. But you're not in it.

JON: Oh yeah.

MADELINE: And then suddenly you show up in there. Your face is in that world. But you're not controlling it. It's your innermost soul, but it's all an act. Then your phone starts ringing.

JON: Oh yeah.

MADELINE: Everybody's got comments.

JON: Exactly.

MADELINE: It's all out of control.

JON: You got that right.

MADELINE: Everybody thinks something about you. Feels something about you. But you don't know what.

JON: Yup.

MADELINE: Your life is an image. That you never meant. And you're dead.

(Pause.)

JON: If I had a nickel for every time that happened to me.

MADELINE: Are you mocking me?

JON: No no oh no no, if you think, let me tell you, the reason I started, what first drew me to magazines, was just that kind of baloney. These eyes are trained weapons. They don't just brush the surface. They plunge the depths. Filter the bad. Grope for the good. When they find it, they yank it out. Into the air. Into the light where it can sizzle and bulge.

MADELINE: I don't think we have the same idea of a nice day.

JON: Try me.

MADELINE: Soft light. Soft breeze. Everybody just moves. Everybody just lives. Everybody just looks straight ahead.

JON: I'm there.

MADELINE: The exact opposite of a sideshow. You know sideshows, right? Clowns poking. Beasts sniffing. Crowds shrieking. Dads yelling.

JON: Sideshows suck.

MADELINE: You won't...tell anyone...the things I say?

JON: Never.

MADELINE: You're very supportive.

JON: I like supporting you.

MADELINE: Being supported lets me get closer to opening up.

JON: I want you to open up.

MADELINE: I'd like to open, sometime.

JON: You can't open here.

MADELINE: Why.

JON: Too open. So I've secured a key to the art room.

MADELINE: Oh.

JON: Meet me there after lunch.

MADELINE: What's there.

JON: Art. Me. Space for supporting.

MADELINE: After lunch...

JON: Tons of support. Tons of gum. You'll open and open and chew and chew and—

(MADELINE *collapses into sleep.*)

JON: Uhh...

(JON *touches* MADELINE'*s shoulder, she wakes.*)

MADELINE: Sorry. New dosage. Mind if I doze?

(She leans on him and closes her eyes.)

ART: *(From down the hall)* Maddy?

MADELINE: *(Eyes closed)* My husband.

(JON'*s body shakes.*)

JON: No meet husband. *(Shaking* MADELINE*)* Make husband go.

(JACKIE *opens her door, sees* JON *shaking* MADELINE, *closes her door.)*

(JON *darts around looking for a hiding place.)*

MADELINE: *(Jerking awake)* If he comes and you're not here what will I say?

ART: *(Getting nearer)* Maddy?

JON: Can't think. Must flee. *(He crawls in circles.)*

(MADELINE *looks for a hiding place, opens the closet.)*

THOMAS: I was sinking into the mud, when—

(MADELINE *closes the closet door and hides behind a table.)*

(ART *enters speaking alternately into a hand-held phone and a small audio recorder.)*

ART: *(To phone)* We're very shaky. Unload debt. Downsize dead weight. Scoop up a silent partner. *(To recorder)* **Press Bob for a merger.** *(To phone)* **Rear-end the raiders before they screw us. Right. Right. Right. Right.**

(JON crawls out the door into the hall. MADELINE comes out from behind a table.)

ART: I thought you were getting your head checked.

MADELINE: All done. He had to step out.

ART: Will you be okay?

MADELINE: Will you be okay.

ART: Drowsy?

MADELINE: No.

ART: Dizzy? Ringing? How your bones.

MADELINE: The dosage is fine.

ART: *(To recorder)* The window in the basement.

MADELINE: Don't forget the heater.

ART: How do I get open the thing.

MADELINE: The heater doesn't have a thing.

ART: The shiny thing. Near the tube. In the box.

MADELINE: You. Don't. Hear. My. Words.

ART: With the rusty edges. The little flame.

MADELINE: God.

ART: Hanging open. Covered with cobwebs. Gushing with sickening fumes, it's a thing.

MADELINE: There is no thing.

ART: *(To recorder)* Cat food. *(To MADELINE)* I took care of the forms.

MADELINE: Drain the plants.

ART: *(To recorder)* Plant closings. *(To MADELINE)* You'll be okay?

MADELINE: The people like me.

ART: Of course they like you. Everybody likes you.

MADELINE: Are you mocking me?

(They stand there.)

ART: I'll be here Tuesday. First thing. What kind of flowers do you want. *(To recorder)* Have Elaine check the deductible.

MADELINE: Everything's ugly falling out of me.

(ART hugs her. She doesn't respond.)

ART: *(To recorder)* Frozen holdings.

MADELINE: What time's your plane.

ART: My plane. What a weekend. Wall to wall meetings right through Monday.

MADELINE: You don't want to have a baby.

ART: I'm trying to build a life worth sharing with another life so you won't have to give up your life.

MADELINE: What life.

ART: *(To recorder)* Have a baby.

MADELINE: Remember the plumber.

ART: I'll be out but I'll leave the keys with the Smiths.

MADELINE: That's not fair. The Smiths will have to stay in so you can go out. It's our plumbing that's messed up. There's nothing wrong with the Smith's plumbing. So you should be the one to stay in. Is the world your colony?

ART: No the world is not my colony. *(To recorder)* Invest in the islands.

MADELINE: What if...I don't know.

ART: What. What.

MADELINE: I. Don't. Know.

(ART *spies gum wrapper.*)

ART: Has someone been buying you gum?

MADELINE: You don't believe I can buy my own gum?

ART: Anything is possible.

MADELINE: I'll walk you to the lobby.

ART: I was going to have my scalp checked.

MADELINE: I told you he stepped out. People don't just appear because you want them.

ART: I'll give him a minute.

MADELINE: I need to get back.

(MADELINE *moves to hug* ART, *but when he moves to hug her she goes.*)

ART: *(To recorder)* Sitting ducks have sore butts.

(THOMAS *comes out of the closet.*)

ART: Oh there you are.

THOMAS: Oh here I really am.

ART: I wonder if you'd do me a favor and take a look at my scalp.

THOMAS: Only if I can tell you my dream.

ART: You're like my dentist.

(THOMAS *rubs* ART'*s head.*)

THOMAS: I was sinking into the mud.

ART: *(To phone)* Cancel my eleven and tell my one o'clock I'm running behind?

THOMAS: I was sinking into the mud.

ART: *(To phone)* Have her meet me where my eleven was supposed to be. I'll call her myself.

THOMAS: I was sinking into the mud and—

ART: *(To* THOMAS*)* The problem started last night, as I
was nodding off I felt this little ping.

THOMAS: I was sinking into the mud.

ART: Middle of the night I woke up scratching, both
hands, hard as I could. The more I scratched the more
it itched, til I was on fire, the back of my head was a
foreign object that scared the shit out of me. I tried to
rip the whole thing off. Hurl it out the window.

THOMAS: I was sinking into the mud, when all of a
sudden, down from the sky came a sparkling—

ART: *(Into phone)* It's me. I can't wait to see you. Call
my office for directions. *(Into recorder)* What am I
doing. *(To* THOMAS*)* What am I doing.

THOMAS: I was sinking into the mud. I couldn't breath.
Then down from the sky came a great big—

ART: Maddy. *(He runs out.)*

THOMAS: *(To nobody)* I was sinking into the. When
down from the. *(He sits.)*Telling a dream to yourself
just isn't good. You've just got to tell it to somebody
who's really not you.

*(*NORMA *enters with a suitcase.)*

NORMA: Are you going to have a nice weekend for me,
Thomas?

THOMAS: Oh I had this really really good dream I just
can't wait to tell you.

NORMA: I have to head out now.

THOMAS: Okay okay but then I get to tell you Monday,
promise?

NORMA: Actually I won't be here Monday. I'm going...
on a vacation.

THOMAS: But I don't want you to go on a vacation.

NORMA: Well, I need to.

THOMAS: But who will take care of me?

NORMA: Other people take care of you all the time.

THOMAS: But not like you.

NORMA: Better than me.

THOMAS: But everybody else wipes me in a hurry and it really hurts.

NORMA: You should tell them to wipe you more slowly.

THOMAS: I do but they just keep wiping in a hurry. When it comes to wiping, you're just the one.

NORMA: You can tell me your dream.

THOMAS: Well, I was sinking into the mud. It was sucking me down. I could hardly breathe. I was stuck there. Then down from the sky there came this sparkling bubble. And then the bubble popped and it turned right into a princess. And she was really really pretty. And she had a really pretty face. And she waved her wand. And it touched my nose. And the sky got all pretty colors. And white birds flew out. And all the mud disappeared. And I was standing there. And I was looking really clean. And I could do all these things with my arms. And so she said let's get married. And we got married and I was really really happy.

NORMA: I like your dream.

THOMAS: I liked it too, so when I woke up I drew a picture of my beautiful princess and just stared and stared. And this is really weird: I kind of knew the face, even though I never saw it before. Do you think I ever really will find someone to marry me?

NORMA: Well, it's never easy.

THOMAS: I would be really really nice to her. All she would have to do is cook me meals two times a day or just one time and wipe my face really slowly. She wouldn't have to stay with me every minute. She could go out every night. She could gossip with her friends. I wouldn't care if she was a great big gossip. I would just want someone to be mine and that would be so nice. Why are you crying?

(NORMA *covers her face.*)

(Unseen by NORMA *and* THOMAS, JACKIE *crawls out from her bedroom holding her sculpture made of found objects. She reaches into the sculpture, pulls out a knife, rises to her feet, moves towards the door, knife drawn.)*

END OF ACT ONE

ACT TWO

Scene 1

(We're in the art room. Door leads to hall. Doors on sides lead to supply closets.)

(The room is cluttered with easels that display patients' paintings. There are also sculptures, some of which are covered.)

(JON charges in circles.)

JON: I'll be going and going. The earth will shake. *(He checks his pocket for gum.)* Spearmint. *(Checks his tie)* Dressed to kill. *(Checks the lock, jiggles it furiously)* Doesn't lock. Of course. Why else would they give Thomas the keys. *(He rages at the door.)* Muh duh buh guh. *(He paces, stops. Pointing to his hand)* You: Assume her shoulder. Win its trust. Clear a path straight across her back. You: *(Pointing to his leg)* Inch over. Make contact. But subtle. Subtle, you hear me? Don't make me pull you aside. You: *(Pointing to his tongue)* luhl luhl luhl. You: *(Pointing to his crotch)* Clean slate. Just be yourself. Feel the music. Think big. *(Pointing to his head)* You: You're going to see some things. On her body. But just let them stand for what they are. Don't start comparing them to things that have nothing to do with the matter at hand. *(He paces.)* Dry run. *(He mimes opening the door, speaking to someone, seating her, putting his arm around her, licking her.)*

(MADELINE *comes in.* JON *jerks around, begins shaking.*)

JON: I was just fuxing up. Fixing up. *(He pretends to straighten up, props an easel against the door, then another, and another, and another, forming a barricade.)*

MADELINE: Why are you propping easels against the door?

JON: Tax purposes.

MADELINE: As I climbed the stairs my head was bunching up but on the top step the shadows let go and my last three years didn't matter.

JON: Spearmint?

(MADELINE *chews.* JON *watches. As she speaks he tries to touch her shoulder, but his hand shakes so violently he has to keep pulling it back.)*

MADELINE: An art room. Like high school. Your heart is so open. Every song seeps into your soul. Why are you nervous?

JON: Ozone layer.

MADELINE: Your arm is shaking.

JON: Right because I lift weights so the massive engines of ligamentation tend to shift into overdrive and vibratitillate.

MADELINE: My husband's still around.

(JON *springs up and runs in circles.)*

MADELINE: I told him I had art therapy, but he might peek in.

JON: Muh duh...

MADELINE: You have no right to be angry at me.

JON: Not angry. Feel great.

MADELINE: Are you nervous because you care...for me?

JON: ...Buh guh...

MADELINE: I think I'm ready to open up.

JON: With your husband down the hall?

MADELINE: Sit.

(JON *sits, shakes.*)

MADELINE: I'm not here now. Not really. What happened was, I did a toothpaste commercial. Let them borrow my soul and that was it. One wrong turn, you know? Bits of me are scattered all over the airwaves. How can I present myself honestly, when there's nothing quite left of me, except this residue with an odor, and a kind of um, what's it called, "loneliness-that-you-can-taste?"

(JON *shrugs.*)

MADELINE: When your mouth is moving but your words are coming from outside the room?

(JON *shrugs.*)

MADELINE: Particles of me still gather near this flesh but I can't make them settle. See? (*Exposing her skin*) Do you see any of Madeline?

JON: Uh, yes?

MADELINE: I think you're wrong. I'm think I'm something in that painting. Do you see me there?

JON: No?

MADELINE: You really see *me* here? (*Her skin*)

JON: Oh yeah.

MADELINE: I think you're right, my self is settling in. Then grab it, quick, before it slips away. I said take me by the skin.

JON: Uh uh...

MADELINE: Is Madeline in your hands?

JON: (*Choked with horror*) It would seem so.

MADELINE: Hold tight. It's a balancing act. If I could just slide the face into place on my skull I'd have Madeline for you. *(She tugs the flesh on her face.)*

JON: Oh, don't bother.

ART: *(Outside)* Maddy?

MADELINE: Keep grabbing me by the skin.

JON: Can I take a rain check?

MADELINE: Don't let go, I'll fly apart.

JON: Rain check. Rain check.

(The door flies open knocking easels over, as ART enters.)

(JON leaps to his feet, drags along MADELINE—who holds his hand on her flesh—to the easel, where he pretends to be an art therapist.)

JON: *(To ART)* Jacques I am Jacques the art therapist, yes I maintain close bond with patient, for your wife she must heal, she must take brush, take aim, and then attack attack attack.

ART: *(To MADELINE)* This guy *(To phone)* Hold on. *(To MADELINE)* is helping you?

(JON guides MADELINE's brush-holding hand so that she keeps painting.)

MADELINE: People in the arts are human.

ART: *(To MADELINE)* Why do you think I don't think people in the arts are human? *(To phone)* One sec.

JON: *(Re. MADELINE's painting)* No no.

MADELINE: Because you're looking at him like you looked at my brother.

JON: No no no no.

ART: *(To MADELINE)* I like your brother.

JON: That is not you that is not true.

MADELINE: When my brother wanted to major in film you said he needed a vacation.

JON: You must dig deeper, deeeeeeeep.

ART: *(To phone)* I'm all yours. *(To* MADELINE*)* I don't need a vacation.

MADELINE: Who said you need a vacation.

ART: *(To phone)* Not you. *(To* MADELINE*)* I'm not taking a vacation.

MADELINE: You're taking a vacation?

ART: *(To* MADELINE*)* I'm not taking a vacation. *(To phone)* Hold on. *(To* MADELINE*)* I'm all yours.

MADELINE: You're taking a vacation.

ART: *(To phone)* I'm not taking a vacation. *(To* MADELINE*)* I'm not having this conversation. I'm heading out to catch my plane and I'm not stopping for anything, except to ask your doctor about this art teacher. *(He exits.)*

JON: I'm a dead man.

MADELINE: Could he be leaving me behind?

*(*JON *darts around, stacks easels against the door.)*

MADELINE: I should ask him. Or not. I should check if the locks have been changed. Am I homeless? *(She starts to drift off to sleep.)*

JON: *(Stops stacking)* What am I doing. I've got to get you out of here.

MADELINE: I need you to hold me. And watch over me. As I sleep. *(She tumbles onto* JON, *asleep.)*

JON: No sleep. *(Shaking her)* As long as you're here he'll come back again and again and a—

*(*THOMAS *enters, knocking over easels.)*

THOMAS: It's your landy-lord.

JON: Oh god.

THOMAS: How's my really best tenant?

JON: You gave me a room that doesn't lock, you idiot.

THOMAS: Since I've been a landy-lord filling up my castle I really think my princess with the white birdies is on her way so I'm going to paint the halls all happy colors.

JON: First help me get Madeline out—No, go keep Jackie downstairs.

THOMAS: But I told Jackie to come *upstairs* to give your new office a scrub.

JON: No no no with Madeline asleep on my lap I can't be seen by—

(JACKIE *enters.* JON *pretends to be checking* MADELINE's *scalp.*)

JON: Jackie. Sedate, huh— Not "it's a date" —She's sedate, it's not a date, just wrapping up— Gum wrappers? (*Stuffing his fingers into gum wrappers*) Better late than never.

THOMAS: He's so silly. (*He exits, painting walls.*)

JACKIE: Don't do it, Jonny.

JON: Do what? What? You think I'd—? With her? Her husband's right down the hall, right Thomas?

(THOMAS *reenters, painting walls.*)

THOMAS: Yup and if you don't believe me see for yourself because he's standing two doors down talking to this thing and that thing.

JON: He's back? Toss me a paint brush.

JACKIE: Why.

JON: Because...

JACKIE: Cause yuh been lying.

JON: No no I said brush because we've got to give him the brush off and rush off because he's a pathetic disgusting sight.

THOMAS: I think he's so cute cause he really likes it when you pet him on the head.

JON: But you shouldn't, he's from incurables. Internal organs about to burst. Struggling to record his last words, it rips your heart out. Everybody into the supply closet.

THOMAS: Oh goody we'll be hiding.

ART: *(Out the door, on phone)* If he tries to screw us...

JON: *(To* JACKIE, *dragging* MADELINE *around)* His own wife can't endure the sight of him, got to get her out of here.

ART: *(Outside the door, on phone)* ...we'll squeeze him til he bleeds.

*(*JON *leaves* MADELINE *on a chair, removes a cover from a sculpture, drapes it over her.)*

JON: Voila. Let's go, Jack.

JACKIE: I won't go in there.

JON: Then go away.

JACKIE: Don't want to.

JON: Then stay here.

JACKIE: Don't want to.

JON: Do what you want. *(He goes into a supply closet.)*

JACKIE: Don't know what I want.

*(*JACKIE *goes into another closet.* THOMAS *tries to follow* JON *into his closet.)*

THOMAS: Can't I hide too?

JON: *(Peeking out)* You stay out and get rid of him. Tell him Jacques is at a cafe having wine with a famous performance artist. *(He goes back into the closet.)*

THOMAS: *(Practices)* Jacques is at a cafe having wine with a famous performance artist. Jacques is at a cafe having wine with a famous performance artist...

(ART enters.)

ART: *(To phone, furious)* I said send my one o'clock where my eleven was *supposed* to be—not where I actually was at eleven. *(Losing control)* So she really is coming to meet me here, in the hospital? *(Takes a deep breath, regains control)* I'll deal with it. *(To* THOMAS*)* Oh it's you. Where's—

THOMAS: In the closet.

ART: What's he doing there?

THOMAS: *(Thinks)* Whining with a famous performance artist.

ART: While I'm waiting for him, could you check me again? *(To recorder)* Cancel check, cancel tennis. *(To* THOMAS*)* I'm about to meet someone very special and those little pings are spreading all over my body.

THOMAS: I'll check your whole body but then I have to straighten up for my princess.

ART: *(To phone)* Bob. I'm about to become unreachable through the weekend, but here's what you've got to do while I'm gone.

(THOMAS checks ART's entire body, removing clothes as necessary. ART talks business, THOMAS misinterprets.)

ART: *(To phone)* It's time to go for it. Take a good look. Closer. Really close. If you see any rough spots smooth them out now. Smooth	THOMAS: My magical princess is on her way. I really really can't wait. *(Examines ART's skin)* When she gets here I'll be

them out or they'll rise up against you. They'll rise up, I'm telling you. Bob. Bob. Don't let them push you. You push them. Don't be afraid to press hard. Fiddle with 'em, you know? See if they jiggle a little. Let things get prickly. Make them sting. Keep looking for a break. Check out the terrain. If they give you an opening take it. There's bound to be a crack. Bob. Bob. Don't be afraid to get your hands dirty. Dig in. Pick away. Make your move before it gets messy. What? Go lower. Lower. Bob. I want you so low they're shaking. Let them shake. If they shake, lick them. Sure you can lick them. I'm not asking, I'm demanding: lick them now. I want you to swallow those guys right up. Chew them up and swallow them down. What are you waiting for? Are you afraid to use your god damn teeth? Devour them now. They're not going anywhere. If they hang in there, cut them off. Cut them right off—but no, don't touch those. Back off completely. Do a dance.

really really happy. (*Rubs*) I'll tidy up and it'll be really tidy. (*Bobs, tweaks, gropes*) There are going to be pretty colors and she'll be really pretty and you should have seen her in my dream, she had a really pretty face and hands and pretty eyes and she was so pretty that I'm going to be so happy, think how happy with those pretty hands and face, that's why everything's just got to be so bright and really pretty just for her. And since she's so really pretty (*Goes lower, bobs*) she gets really pretty things all around her every single day. Anyway I saw her in a dream and I'm going to be so happy every little day (*Licks*) because she'll be oh so really nice to me all the time she'll be really nice. I can just feel her on the way, I can tell she's really coming because (*Chews*) can't you just sometimes tell when something's about to happen, (*Considers cutting*) you know you can sometimes tell? (*Dances,*

That's right. Keep our butt *puts* ART's *clothes back on)* covered. I don't want so I have to get everything anything left hanging in really neat and really the wind. Keep dancing. pretty so I really have That's it. Yeah. Dance. to go now bye bye bye. Right. Later. *(He goes.)*

ART: *(To phone)* I'm checking about flowers I ordered. "I'm crazy for you my Melody". *(Losing control)* I said I need them on the sixth floor by one, not the first floor by six. *(Takes a deep breath, regains control)* Then cancel the order.

(JACKIE *peeks out of her closet.)*

ART: *(To himself)* The famous performance artist who was whining with Jacques. I hate weird theater.

(JACKIE *moves around the room, towards the door to the hall.)*

JACKIE: *(Observing* ART, *to herself)* Internal organs about to burst, just like Jonny said. Incurable. Doomed.

ART: *(To recorder)* It's like she sees stuff nobody else can see...

JACKIE: Those shoes tomorrow: empty? Body: rotting? Weeds on his face.

ART: *(To recorder, moved)* ...and she really feels what she's saying...so I feel it too.

(JACKIE *in grief, grunts, drools)*

ART: *(To recorder, even more moved)* Messy, but true.

JACKIE: Talking to nobody.

ART: *(To recorder, verge of tears)* Aren't we all.

JACKIE: *(Moved)* So pointless. So gross.

ART: *(Weeps aloud)* Yes. Yes.

JACKIE: *(Verge of tears)* I'm looking at a guy who's gone.

(JACKIE *howls, embraces* ART. JON *peeks out of his closet.*)

ART: Bravo.

(As JACKIE *tears herself away and exits,* ART *sees* JON.*)*

ART: *(To* JON*)* Hey, get out here.

JON: Too busy.

ART: I didn't come to hassle you, the doctor told me the art therapists really do help the patients.

JON: They do. We do. Help.

ART: I need to know where my wife is.

JON: I would try the other end of the building.

ART: I don't want to find her. I just want to make sure she's not here, since there was a mix up and my new girlfriend's coming to meet me here. *(To recorder)* Meat. Freezer.

(JON *darts around.*)

JON: Girlfriend coming here.

ART: *(To* JON*)* Maddy and me have been arguing constantly. That's not a life. *(To recorder)* Cereal. *(To* JON*)* You okay? You're jumping around like you've got to go to the bathroom.

JON: I'm part Indonesian.

ART: I'm not saying anything about the affair to Maddy, in case it doesn't pan out. *(To recorder)* Bacon. *(To* JON*)* I'm just testing the waters. You've been in this situation before, I'm sure, being an artist.

JON: We artists, always testing each other's waters.

ART: *(Joking)* Just so you don't test Maddy's waters.

JON: *(Laughing)* Right right right.

ART: Oh, if I found her with another guy I'd be fine.

JON: *(Laughing)* Sure sure sure.

ART: *(Laughs)* He wouldn't.

JON: *(Laughs, hysterically, til he can hardly breathe)*

(THOMAS enters with a mop and bucket, laughs along.)

THOMAS: *(To JON)* I told you he was fun. *(To ART)* He said you were "a pathetic disgusting sight". Tee hee.

ART: *(To JON)* The guy who checks heads is really out to lunch, isn't he.

JON: He sure am. Is.

THOMAS: *(Leaving off wax)* So here's Jackie's cleaning stuff, I'll be downstairs bringing my princess' picture upstairs. *(Sees MADELINE)* What a heavy sleeper—

(JON pushes THOMAS out.)

JON: —sculpture, yes, very heavy sculpture.

ART: You can get back to whatever, Melody'll be here any minute.

(MADELINE stirs under the cover.)

JON: I better get a box for Maddy's body. Of work.

(JON goes into the other supply closet, as NORMA enters through the main door, dressed in street clothes and blue scarf, carrying suit case, smiling.)

ART: There's the smile that makes me feel like I'm flying. Melody.

(ART embraces NORMA.)

NORMA: *(Aside)* I needed a name that was more melodic.

ART: The flowers I ordered didn't make it. But it's the thought that counts, and I've been thinking about this trip every minute of the week.

NORMA: Me too. *(Smiles)*

ART: Our car will be a few minutes.

NORMA: No problem.

(JACKIE *enters,* NORMA *hides behind a painting,* JACKIE *grabs bucket.)*

ART: *(To* JACKIE*)* Bravo.

(JACKIE *drops bucket, hurries out,* NORMA *comes out of hiding.)*

ART: Sorry to make you meet me here, I had to stop by because we're bidding on a company that makes a hot new medication.

NORMA: Which one?

ART: Oh, it's called, uh—

NORMA: Not that I would know—

ART: *(Struggles to make up a name)* flora—

NORMA: —anything about—

ART: —tri-something—

NORMA: —anything. *(Giggles hysterically)*

(JON *comes out of the supply closet with a large box.)*

JON: Norma?

ART: Norma?

NORMA: *(To* ART*)* They call me Melody, Mel, Melo, Norma...

ART: How do you know someone who works here?

NORMA: I'll tell you after you check if the car's here.

(NORMA *hands* ART *her suitcase and hurries him away.)*

ART: I'll check if the car's here. *(He goes.)*

NORMA: When he comes back you've got to call me Melody.

JON: He can't come back.

NORMA: You don't like him, from one look?

JON: He looks like someone I hate: him.

NORMA: I finally met a guy who's decent and single...

JON: 0 for 2.

NORMA: ...so if you could just—

JON: *(Flying into a rage)* I want him out out out out—

NORMA: We'll be gone in a minute if you'll help me think up an explanation for how I know you, a patient who—

JON: Not patient. Art therapist.

NORMA: Right right. So you're an art therapist. Who I know through your girlfriend, an actress named Madeline who went to drama school near my business school.

JON: Don't tell him actress Madeline my girlfriend. Madeline no girlfriend. Actress no Madeline.

(MADELINE wakes, throws off the cover.)

MADELINE: *(To JON)* You're mocking me, with her?

NORMA: *(To MADELINE)* I know you.

JON: *(To MADELINE)* She works here.

NORMA: *(To MADELINE)* I don't work here.

JON: *(To MADELINE)* Doesn't work here.

MADELINE: *(Clinging to JON)* I need you to stick with me.

JON: I'm having trouble sticking to myself.

NORMA: *(To JON)* This is your actress?

JON: Not mine, not actress.

MADELINE: I'm not an actress?

JON: No. Yes.

MADELINE: *(Touching NORMA's scarf)* She's taken my look.

NORMA: *(Touching* MADELINE's *lips)* I know her face.

MADELINE: And now she's taken my friend.

NORMA: *(To* MADELINE*)* I didn't come for Jon. I came for this guy I'm seeing. I'll introduce you.

JON: *(To* NORMA*)* Don't introduce. *(To* MADELINE*)* Don't see.

NORMA & MADELINE: Why?

JON: Because—

*(*ART *enters with* NORMA's *suitcase, puts his arm around her.* JON *drops the box over* MADELINE*.)*

NORMA: *(To* ART*)* I want you to meet Jon who's an art therapist here, and this is—

*(*MADELINE *throws off the box.)*

ART: My wife.

MADELINE: My husband.

*(*MADELINE *charges* ART*.)*

*(*ART *drops* NORMA's *bag and passes her to* JON*.)*

NORMA: My life.

*(*JACKIE *enters, sees* NORMA *clinging to* JON*.)*

JACKIE: My Jonny.

JON: *(To* JACKIE, *re* NORMA*)* My girlfriend?

*(*JACKIE *pulls out her knife and tries to stab herself.)*

*(*THOMAS *enters with a crayon drawing of his princess— who looks exactly like Melody/the new Norma, with blue scarf, etc.)*

THOMAS: *(Admiring the drawing)* My beautiful princess—

*(*JON *passes* NORMA *to* THOMAS, *grapples with* JACKIE*.)*

THOMAS: *(Seeing* NORMA*)* —has arrived!

*(*THOMAS *lifts up* NORMA *in his arms.)*

(NORMA's bag falls open. The bag is completely empty, except for the image of white birds in a blue sky. We hear the sound of birds.)

(NORMA screams.)

(ART's recorder starts playing, his phone starts ringing, and all six characters speak at once:)

JACKIE: I saw yuh Jonny. It's done now Jonny.

JON: Get down. Get out. Don't look. Don't see.

ART: *(To* MADELINE*)* I'm all yours. *(To phone)* I'm all yours. *(To* MADELINE*)* I'm all yours. *(To phone)* I'm all yours.

MADELINE: You cut me open and I'm ugly falling out of all the particles that scattered from my face across the

THOMAS: She's my beautiful princess and I'll be so happy forever and ever.

(NORMA *screams.*)

(End of scene)

Scene 2

(Back in the common room)

(ART's *jacket hangs on the wall. Beside it, wrapped flowers with a note.)*

(ART, JACKIE, *and* JON *sit, bound in straight jackets.* MADELINE *sits, hands and feet loosely chained to the wall. In their various states of unconsciousness, these four characters mutter sporadic unintelligible phrases.)*

(NORMA *sits on the floor in fetal position, rocking.)*

(Suddenly NORMA *springs to her feet, starts to remove clothing as she charges out.)*

(Though the other characters are still unconscious, their muttering becomes intelligible:)

JON: Get down.

MADELINE: My...

JON: Don't look.

MADELINE: ...face.

JACKIE: Stop.

(Silence.)

ART: Sinking. Kicking.

(JACKIE mumbles.)

JON: Get get get get get get get get

MADELINE: Particles.

ART: Kick in the

JON:	JACKIE:	(MADELINE
Don't.	Don't.	*gasps.)*

(They become quiet. THOMAS enters.)

THOMAS: Oh Jon my princess came and now I just can't find her—

JON: *(Still unconscious)* Get down.

THOMAS: She was Norma but she was all dressed in—

JON: Get out.

THOMAS: He's haloosirnating. *(To MADELINE)* My princess came and she was—

(MADELINE wails.)

THOMAS: She's haloosirnating too. *(To JACKIE)* Oh Jackie my princess came, and you'll never guess who—

JACKIE: Stop.

THOMAS: —she—

JACKIE: I said.

THOMAS: —was.

JACKIE: Stop.

THOMAS: Cattertonic. Try try again. *(To* ART*)* Down
from the sky, she was—

*(*ART *snores.)*

THOMAS: Fast asleep. This is like when I really wanted
to tell my dad things but he was dead, but the priest
said his body's right there so just tell him, so I did
but it really didn't help because when I need to tell
somebody things they just can't be haloosirnating or
cattertonic or fast asleep or dead. I'm a perfectionist.

*(*THOMAS *waits near the door, looking out.* MADELINE *and*
JACKIE *begin to awaken.)*

MADELINE: *(Half asleep)* He had someone else. Standing
where I stand. He cut me out...

JACKIE: He did it.

MADELINE: *(Awake)* ...of my own life.

JACKIE: *(Awake)* He just. Did it.

MADELINE: We seem to have a lot in common.

*(*JACKIE *sobs, stops.)*

MADELINE: Did someone cut you out of your own life?

JACKIE: *(Nods vigorously)*

MADELINE: With the swiftness of a—

*(*JACKIE *nods vigorously.)*

MADELINE: —and this after years of cramming his
asinine dictates all over your—

JACKIE: Chair.

MADELINE: —to the point where every time you try to
open up he's right there with his—

JACKIE: Chair.

MADELINE: —making it completely impossible for you
to—

JACKIE: Magazines.

MADELINE: Exactly.

JACKIE: And so near my teeth.

MADELINE: So let's do something about it.

JACKIE: I got to strike myself, soon's I find my knife.

MADELINE: Why turn your anger inward? Trust your impulse. Take action. Strike him.

JACKIE: Huh.

MADELINE: Where's your knife.

(JACKIE *shakes her head.*)

MADELINE: Any other utensils?

JACKIE: *(Thinks)* Fork.

MADELINE: Excellent. Where.

JACKIE: *(Calls to* THOMAS*)* Hey.

(THOMAS *turns to face them.*)

JACKIE: *(To* THOMAS*)* Under my bed, in my sculpture, there's a fork.

THOMAS: If I get it can I tell you about my princess?

JACKIE: No.

THOMAS: I'll get it anyway.

(THOMAS *goes into* JACKIE's *room.*)

MADELINE: This is a big step for you.

(THOMAS *returns, puts a fork in* JACKIE's *mouth.*)

THOMAS: If anybody wants me...

(THOMAS *returns to the door, faces out.* MADELINE *takes the fork from* JACKIE's *mouth.*)

MADELINE: And now I strike my husband.

JACKIE: Him?

MADELINE: Why not.

JACKIE: Already...sick?

MADELINE: Very. What makes me sick is—

JACKIE: First strike the other one.

MADELINE: Him?

JACKIE: Why not.

MADELINE: Seems so...sweet.

JACKIE: He'd been showering her with gum.

MADELINE: If he hurt you, he should be stricken. But first I'll strike my husband, finally get through. Or not. It's your call.

JACKIE: *(Slipping into trance)* Got to hibernate.

MADELINE: *(Starting to doze)* Should we forget it?

JACKIE: If yuh don't, they'll just keep doing what they do...

MADELINE: You're right. It's time.

(JACKIE *slips into a trance.*)

(MADELINE *leans towards* ART *with the fork, reaching as far as the chains will allow her: inches from his face.*)

(MADELINE *falls asleep with the fork clenched in her fist, right above* ART'*s face.*)

(ART *wakes, sees the fork at his face, screams.* MADELINE *sways towards* JON. JON *wakes, sees the fork at his face, screams.*)

ART: Why the hell didn't you tell me Maddy was in your art room?

JON: I was shocked.

ART: How could you not know somebody was in that room?

JON: Cause she was hiding, ashamed, of her love, for
art class. When you mentioned your girlfriend was
coming I begged her to run, to fly, to—

ART: Then you knew she was there.

JON: I did?

ART: You said you tried to get her to run.

JON: Right.

ART: If you knew she was there why didn't you tell me.

JON: Because. Distracted. When I saw Norma.

ART: Melody.

JON: Melody. Right. Old friend. School friend.
Met her through a girlfriend, actress named
Madubuduhduhduh.

ART: However you did it you really screwed up, so
you've got to help me out with Maddy.

JON: Anything.

ART: Say Melody came to see you, because you and
Melody have been going out.

JON: No problem. Yes problem. It would hurt Jackie,
who's right there.

ART: The performance artist.

JON: We've been tasting each other's waters.

ART: So that's why she blew up when she saw you
holding Melody.

JON: She blew up, right, because she counts on me.
Devoted. Scrubs with every ounce, every muscle, every
tissue, so I can walk on pure floor. She makes our floor
a sky. Pure sky drips from her hands. But I filth it up.
I filth it, just show up, and my actions, they take off
and do stuff. I try to grab hold of my actions but even
that becomes actions and before you know it I'm just a

glop of jelly swarming with actions. She's grace. Pure sky but I'm tiny, a big wet tiny, a squid with nothing to clutch onto, my one rock is her but I blew it up and there's nothing I can say. I'm so disgusted with my actions I can hardly breathe. *(Panting)*

ART: In other words, you really like her.

(JON nods.)

ART: So if we can prove Melody's seeing some other guy, we'll save both our asses, right?

(JON nods.)

ART: But if we can't say it's you, and we can't say it's me, who can we get to go along with our story?

JON: *(Calls to* THOMAS*)* Hey.

(THOMAS turns around.)

ART: There's nobody else?

JON: We're working with a very small talent pool.

THOMAS: So can I tell you what happened?

JON: We need you to be in our play.

THOMAS: Oh goody goody.

JON: All you have to do is, make believe a woman came to see you this afternoon.

THOMAS: A woman did come to see me this afternoon.

JON: Perfect.

ART: Really she came to see me, but you have to keep saying—

THOMAS: Oh no she came to see me.

ART: Right. And she works in a bank.

THOMAS: No she doesn't.

JON: Make believe, Thomas.

THOMAS: A bank. Make believe.

ART: She really goes for you because you're...

JON: Why would she go for him?

ART: Because...he has a quality that she...

THOMAS: I have no quality.

JON: She craves him because...

ART: Because...

THOMAS: Maybe she just doesn't know.

(MADELINE *stirs.*)

JON: Doesn't know.

ART: Feelings took her by surprise.

JON: Go with that.

THOMAS: But the really weird thing is, after she came all the way to see me, when I held her in my arms she only screamed and screamed.

ART: That they'll believe.

THOMAS: And then I couldn't find her.

ART: She came, they embraced, she ran screaming from the building.

JON: Bingo.

THOMAS: (*Leaving*) You think she's maybe running away?

ART: Where you going?

JON: It's show time.

(THOMAS *tries to leave,* ART *and* JON *block his way.*)

THOMAS: But my princess might be running away and I've really really waited so long.

(THOMAS *escapes.* JON *and* ART *fall on* MADELINE *and* JACKIE, *waking them.*)

ART: Maddy.

JON: Jackie.

MADELINE: *(To* ART*)* Keep your words off my brain.

(JACKIE *hisses at* JON*.)*

ART: The woman you saw me with—

MADELINE: *(Screams to drown him out)* AAAAAAAAA.

JON: She didn't come to see me.

(JACKIE *hisses.)*

(All 4, simultaneously:)

ART: She came to see Thomas. The guy who was standing there. His name is Thomas. *(To* JON*)* What are you saying? *(To* MADELINE*)* She came to see Thomas—	JON: She didn't come to see me it was him, Norma came to see this guy *(Indicates* ART*)* him him him him— *(Responding to* ART*)* I mean Thomas Thomas Thomas Thomas—
MADELINE: *(Screams repeatedly)* AAAAA...	(JACKIE *hisses repeatedly.)*

*(*ART *and* JON *give up, droop to the ground, exhausted. Pause)*

MADELINE: Thomas?

ART: That's right, it was him.

JON: She really did she came for Thomas.

(THOMAS *enters carrying the clothes* NORMA *wore as Melody.)*

THOMAS: No I think she really didn't come for me because people don't really come for me, I just dream they do because look, she burst, just like a dream.

ART: What he means is...

JON: They embraced.

ART: She ran screaming.

JON: She ran miles from the building.

(NORMA *enters, dressed in hospital uniform again.*)

NORMA: No I didn't.

ART: Why are you here?

NORMA: I don't know. This afternoon I thought I was dropping by to escape. The path was clear. With Jon playing an artist, my lie was airtight. I was inches from freedom. Then I lost control, went plunging through someone else's dream, til I crashed into a new place where I was ripped open, pierced with feelings triggered not by my thoughts, but the thoughts of another. Thomas. What hurts you hurts me. What thrills you thrills me. It's glorious. It's creepy. I don't know what it is. I don't know anything. Why I plan. Why I gesture. Why the weight shifts around on my feet and moisture pops out on my shoulders. Why my lips shift into different shapes when my eyes notice certain hands and then words come. I don't know what the earth has to do with me or what my bones have to do with my thoughts. But I know that you have to do with me. I'm hooked. I'm here. I'm not alone.

(NORMA *frees* JACKIE, MADELINE, ART, *and* JON, *while humming a passionate melody.*)

THOMAS: (*Pinching himself*) Pinchy pinchy. My cheeks aren't dreaming. Pinchy pinchy. My legs aren't dreaming. Oh Jon. My princess really did come and she turned right into Norma. And all because you set up a really fun office where magical things could happen.

NORMA: (*To* THOMAS) Time to wash up for bed.

THOMAS: Will you tell me a story?

NORMA: When your hair is all brushed, and your neck is all scrubbed, and your room is all tidied up, I will tell you a fairy tale.

(THOMAS *yelps for glee.*)

(THOMAS *and* NORMA *exit.*)

(JACKIE *crawls to her room.* JON *takes off his tie, sits, stares at a magazine, his energy level plunging.*)

MADELINE: So she's a hospital worker, who left. Then came back. To see Thomas.

ART: And the art teacher is a patient, who acted like an artist, to help the hospital worker. Somehow.

(MADELINE *kicks a chair.*)

ART: What.

MADELINE: If your excuse fell apart, I wouldn't have to keep seeing you and hearing you.

ART: Why don't you want to see and hear me?

MADELINE: Because I'm trying, with all my might, to squirm back into my life. Your words mess up my concentration.

ART: If we don't talk we get nowhere.

MADELINE: If we don't talk we get nowhere, if we do talk we get nowhere.

ART: Can I stay the night?

(MADELINE *shakes her head.*)

ART: *(To recorder)* Cut out late calls. Make marriage work. *(Smashing the audio recorder)* Keep trying. *(Smashes)* Keep trying. *(Smashes. To* MADELINE*)* Now can I stay the night?

(*She shakes her head, gets his jacket from the door, notices the wrapped flowers.*)

ART: Oh Jeez. They delivered the flowers to the first floor at six instead of the sixth floor at one. I'm nailed. Don't read it, Maddy. I wasn't me. I was a child. Maybe I am a child. I'm a child, Maddy. But without

you I don't have a face. Or legs. I have no face and no
legs without you Maddy.

MADELINE: *(Reads)* "Mad. For you. My melody."
(Moved) I'm your melody? How did you learn to write
poetry?

ART: It just came.

*(MADELINE reaches her hand out to ART. He takes her hand.
Hands joined, they exit.)*

(JACKIE crawls out, scrubbing.)

JACKIE: It's a lie. Isn't it.

JON: What.

JACKIE: The whole day.

JON: Can't even remember.

JACKIE: Why do yuh lie to me, Jonny.

(JON shrugs.)

JACKIE: Yuh don't even know.

(JON shrugs.)

JACKIE: I lived on twigs. I lived on garbage. I lived on a
soaked piece of cardboard. But I'd rather have nothing
than you. Cause yuh don't know a single thing.

JON: I do.

JACKIE: What.

JON: It's something...I can't say.

JACKIE: How come.

(JON shrugs.)

JACKIE: Say it.

(JON's whole body shakes)

JACKIE: What.

JON: This is it.

(JON puts his hand near JACKIE's shoulder. It shakes violently and he pulls it away.

(NORMA *enters carrying a tray of pills, observes as:*)

(JON *stands before* JACKIE, *and struggles to present a dance. Though it's jerky and awkward, it's the best he can do.*)

JON: It's about you.

(JON *dances,* JACKIE *sways.*)

END OF PLAY